# Nature's Children

# SWANS

**Tim Harris**

GROLIER

# FACTS IN BRIEF

## Classification of Swans

Class: *Aves* (birds)
Order: *Anseriformes*
Family: *Anatidae* (ducks, geese, and swans)
Genus: There are two swan genera, *Coscoroba* and *Cygnus*.
Species: There are seven species of swans.

**World distribution.**  Swans live in the tropical, temperate, and polar regions of North and South America, Europe, Asia, and Australasia.

**Habitat.**  Swans always live close to water—mostly fresh water in rivers, lakes, and swamps. Many also live on ponds in city parks.

**Distinctive physical characteristics.**  Large. Long neck with wedge-shaped beak. Strong legs. Webbed feet. Brilliant white or black plumage.

**Habits.**  Good swimmers and fliers. Walk slowly on land.

**Diet.**  Mostly plant material—including grass and underwater plants. Also some small animals (mute swan).

© 2004 The Brown Reference Group plc
Printed and bound in U.S.A.
Edited by John Farndon and Angela Koo

**Published by:**

**An imprint of Scholastic
Library Publishing
Old Sherman Turnpike, Danbury,
Connecticut 06816**

**Library of Congress Cataloging-in-Publication Data**
Harris, Tim.
    Swans / Tim Harris.
        p. cm. — (Nature's children)
    Includes index.
    Summary: Describes the physical characteristics, habits, and habitats of swans.
    ISBN 0–7172–5957–9 (set)        ISBN 0–7172–5974–9
    1. Swans—Juvenile literature. [1. Swans.] I. Title. II. Series.

QL696.A52H36 2004
598.4'18—dc21

2003049178

# Contents

A swimming mute swan is one of the most beautiful birds. Its white feathers gleam. Its neck is long and graceful. Its wings arch elegantly over its back. People have admired swans for hundreds of years. The famous writer William Shakespeare wrote about their beauty more than 400 years ago. The first Europeans who went to Australia, South Africa, and North America enjoyed watching swans so much that they took some with them. Swans now live in all these places.

There is more to swans than beauty, though. Some swans can fly nonstop for thousands of miles. Swans can fly as high as a cruising jet plane. Swan couples remain loyal to each other throughout their lifetime. They are caring parents and can be tough fighters when it comes to defending their young.

*Mute swans are the largest and most beautiful of swans. When they swim on the water, they arch their wings and neck gracefully. This one's wings are especially arched in order to deter an intruder.*

# Birds of the Water

Opposite page:
*Swans graze on water plants. They bend their long necks down into the water to nip off juicy greenery.*

All swans are big birds. The largest swan, the mute swan, is the world's heaviest flying bird. It can weigh 50 pounds (22 kilograms). That's as much as eight Christmas turkeys! Despite their size, swans are graceful birds with long, curving necks. Most swans are covered with startlingly white feathers. Some are jet black.

Swans are strong fliers and can fly long distances. When they fly, their wings beat slowly and their great necks stretch in front of them. But being so big makes it hard to get airborne. And it is on the water that swans are really at home. They swim well, paddling with webbed feet. You can't see the feet moving underwater, so they seem to glide effortlessly.

A swan's neck is perfect for reaching down into the water to nip off underwater plants. Sometimes swans come ashore to eat grass, but their webbed feet make them waddle awkwardly. When danger threatens, though, they may flap their wings wildly to help them break into a kind of run.

# Meet the Family

Swans are not the only birds to live mostly on water. They are part of the waterfowl family, along with ducks and geese. Bird experts call the family Anatidae (said an-AT-ee-die.) There are more than 140 types of waterfowl. They live almost anywhere there is fresh water—on lakes, rivers, swamps, even mountain streams.

Some waterfowl are tiny; the biggest are among the biggest of all birds. But all are very much at home on water. They are strong swimmers, paddling along with webbed feet and kept dry by waterproof feathers. Chicks can swim just a few hours after hatching. Because stretches of water can be far apart, most waterfowl are strong fliers, too.

Life in the water can be chilly. So waterfowl keep themselves warm with a coat of fluffy down under their feathers and a thick layer of fat under the skin. Waterfowl are perfectly suited to feeding in water. They have long necks for stretching down into the water and flat bills for sifting out food.

Opposite page: *These are smaller relatives of swans called black-bellied whistling ducks. Like swans, they have long necks and an upright pose.*

# A World of Swans

There are seven types, or species, of swans. If you live in a city, the swans you see are likely to be mute swans, since they make their homes even on city-center lakes and ponds.

Tundra swans build their nests and raise their families in barren areas around the Arctic Ocean in the far north of Canada and Russia. The tundra swans of Eurasia are different from their North American cousins and are called Bewick's swans. Trumpeter swans spend their summer in similar places or on lakes and swamps in the huge forests of the far north. Those regions become very cold in winter, so in fall the tundra and trumpeter swans fly thousands of miles south to warmer areas.

Black-necked and coscoroba swans live on lakes surrounded by tall grasses and sedges in South America. Black swans live in similar types of places in Australia. Although swans live in many regions, you never see one on the open oceans, in dense forests and woodland, or in deserts or anywhere far from water.

*Black-necked swans are small swans that live on lakes and rivers in South America.*

# Fantastic Feathers

Like all birds, swans are covered in feathers. Feathers are amazing. They keep a bird warm and dry. They are strong enough to support the swan when it is flying. Yet they are light enough not to bring the bird crashing back to the ground. A swan's feathers have to be particularly strong since swans are big birds.

Next time you see a feather lying on the ground, take a closer look. It is made of a long, pointed part, called a shaft, and a thin, flat section called a vane that is made up of hundreds of tiny barbs. One feather on its own is not very tough, but a bird's wing has layer on layer of feathers that make the wing very strong. The air trapped between the layers keeps the bird nice and warm—as fur does on a rabbit or cat—and special oil on the feathers keeps them dry when the swan is swimming.

Opposite page: *This swan is preening—keeping its feathers in tiptop condition. As it preens, the swan uses its bill to straighten and untangle ruffled feathers. It may smear a little oil on, too, from a special organ under its tail.*

13

# Dropping Like Feathers

Opposite page:
*These young mute swans are not dirty; they are molting. Soon, the brown and gray feathers will be replaced by pure white ones.*

Although feathers are fantastic, they don't last forever. They suffer a lot of wear and tear. Every time a swan flies, bumps into a plant, or has a fight with another swan, the delicate vanes are damaged, and they cannot be repaired. A swan with damaged feathers would eventually die. It would not be able to fly, so enemies could attack it. And it would have no protection against the cold and wet.

Swans get around that problem by changing their old feathers for new ones every year. This is called molting. The old feathers don't all drop out at once, though. If they did, the swan would look like a plucked chicken and would probably freeze to death! Instead, different feathers are molted at different times. Mute swans replace their wing feathers in July and August, and at this time the birds cannot fly.

# Not All White

Seen from a distance, most swans look all bright white. The exceptions are the black swan and the black-necked swan. As its name suggests, the black swan is mostly black, but it has big white patches on its wings. The black-necked swan has a white body, but it looks as if it has a black sock over its neck.

Get a little closer to a swan, and you will see more color. Most swans have yellow, orange, or red on their bills. Mute swans have a black knob on top of their orange bills. South American black-necked swans have a red knob on their bills. The coscoroba swan has a bright red bill and pink legs.

*No swan is completely white or black. Like all mute swans, this one has an orange bill topped with a nob of black and tipped with black.*

## Beakprints

Could you tell one individual swan from another? Probably not. But scientists have found a way. Just as the police can identify a person by looking at the pattern of their fingerprints, so swan experts can tell individual Bewick's swans apart just by looking at their bill patterns.

Each Bewick's swan has a different bill pattern. Some have more black. Others have more yellow. The pattern may help the swans tell each other apart. Identifying individual swans also helps swan experts find out about the swans' habits.

Swan experts watched the swans that returned to a bird preserve in England every fall. They discovered that the same birds returned year after year, after flying thousands of miles from the far north. After a while the experts got to know some individuals and even gave them names.

# A Bite to Eat

Swans are mostly herbivores. That means they eat plant matter. Favorite snacks include leaves, shoots, roots, and grass. Mute swans do eat a few animals as well, including frogs, toads, tadpoles, mollusks, worms, and insects.

Swans may eat in the water or on land. If swimming, they either dip just their head and neck underwater to pull up plants, or they upend. Upending is when the swan plunges right into the water so only its tail sticks up. That way it can reach deeper for food. Water is often muddy, so if you see a swan with a mucky neck, you know that it's been upending! Sometimes, swans paddle their legs in the water to stir up tasty morsels.

On land swans rip off bits of plant material with their bill. Sometimes they dig in the soil to get at a hidden root. They usually dig with their bill, but for extratough roots they use their large feet as well.

*Because it is such a big bird, a mute swan needs
a long runup before it can take off from the water.*

# Taking to the Air

A fully grown swan weighs about the same as an infant child. So it has to be strong to get airborne! A swan cannot lift off from a standstill. Instead, it takes a long runup, like a plane on an airport runway. For their runway swans can use water or land. When it takes off from water, the swan runs along the surface, splashing its feet, beating its wings, and making lots of noise. When it is going fast enough, it rises into the air and climbs slowly, beating its wings. Coscoroba swans have longer legs than other swans. So they can run faster than other swans and take off quicker.

Swans fly fast and very high in the sky when they are on long journeys. Tundra, trumpeter, whooper, and mute swans can fly as fast as a cruising automobile, at 50–60 miles per hour (80–96 kilometers per hour). They can also fly very high. A group of whooper swans was once tracked by radar as it flew over Ireland at 27,000 feet (8,200 meters)— almost as high as a cruising jet plane.

# Out of the Freezer

Opposite page:
*Winter is too cold in Finland for whooper swans to stay all year round. This pair has arrived back from the south after the winter—only to find themselves caught in a late snowstorm.*

Many swans live in places where they cannot find food all year round. Tundra and trumpeter swans spend summer in the tundra in the far north of Alaska, Canada, and Russia. In summer there is lots of plant matter for the swans to eat both on land and in the tundra's many ponds. But in fall the weather there turns bitterly cold. Blizzards cover the ground in snow. Lakes and ponds freeze over. And the swans cannot get at their food. To find food, they must fly far south every fall to warmer places. This long journey is called migration.

As the weather warms up the following spring, the swans fly north to the tundra again. They arrive just as the weather is getting warmer and the plants that they eat start to grow once more. No one knows how the swans decide the time is right to make their long flight. Not all swans migrate. Some don't have to fly to warmer places because they can get all the food they need where they live.

# Bird's-eye View

Flying all the way from Alaska to California to avoid the bitter cold of winter is very tiring for tundra swans. So before they set off, they eat as much as they can to give them energy on the journey. Swans do not migrate alone; they fly with their friends. Tundra swans fly higher and higher until they reach a cruising height thousands of feet above the ground. Tundra swans flying from Alaska fly day and night until they reach the Great Salt Lake in Utah. After a brief stopover they take off again, this time flying over the Sierra Mountains into California, where they spend the winter. Tundra swans that breed in northern Canada follow a different route, flying over Hudson Bay south to the coast around Chesapeake Bay, in Maryland and Virginia.

*Like all swans, mute swans can fly powerfully and far. If you have sharp ears, you can actually hear a throbbing sound as their strong wings beat the air.*

# Flocking Together

Swans often stick together. When they molt their flight feathers and cannot fly, they gather in hundreds or even thousands for safety. A gathering of swans like that is called a herd. The molting swans stay together on lakes or ponds until they can fly again. Sometimes swans join up in big groups when they migrate in spring and fall. In winter swans may often herd together to graze grassy fields.

Why do they spend so much time together? One reason is that they probably like each other's company. Another reason is that in a group there are more pairs of eyes to watch for enemies. A swan feeding on its own could easily fall prey to a hunting animal. In a herd of several hundred swans there will always be a few with their heads up, watching for danger.

*Whooper swans like these often gather in large herds by lakes where there is plenty of food.*

# It's Nice to Talk

Most swans are very talkative. They call to each other to tell of good food or danger. They shout to scare off enemies, and courting couples speak to each other. They make a whole range of sounds, from a noise like a dog's bark to a wild hissing.

Mute means silent, and the mute swan is the quietest of the swans. Quiet, that is, until a dog or a person approaches its eggs or babies. Then it will loudly hiss to defend its young family.

Other swans can often be much noisier. The coscoroba swan is named for its "cos-cor-oo" call, which sounds rather like a toy trumpet. Tundra swans honk and yelp to each other when they swim and when they take to the air. Trumpeter swans sound like distant bugles when they shout their low-pitched "ko-hoh." Swans can be a noisy bunch; but when they are feeding, they are usually quieter.

Opposite page:
*When its young are threatened, a mute swan may throw its head up and hiss loudly. It may even make a bark like a puppy dog's.*

# Back Off!

Opposite page:
*At breeding time, male mute swans fiercely defend their own territory. If another male intrudes, the two may fight like this. One swan usually backs off quietly after a while. But sometimes the fight is to the death.*

During the breeding season mute swans become very aggressive toward outsiders and sometimes to other swans. Any animal or person coming too close to the nest may be scolded or even attacked. A curious dog, for example, might not know any better and try to approach a swan's nest with eggs in it. If so, the mom and dad swans make scary hissing noises, arch their wing feathers over their back, fluff out the feathers on their neck, and bend their necks back. Then the dog would probably back away. If it came any closer, one or other of the swans would move toward it.

Sometimes a swan will fight to the death to keep an intruder away. Swans do not want to pick a fight, but are very brave in defending their young ones. At other times of the year, when there are no eggs or chicks, swans simply swim, walk, or fly away from trouble.

*Swan upping on the Thames River in England, when mute swans are caught and marked with their owners' stamp.*

# Royal Swans

People have admired swans' beauty for hundreds of years. In some places rich people kept mute swans as pets to show off to their friends. They also discovered that swans were good to eat. They looked after them, kept them well fed, and cooked them for special occasions, such as royal banquets. The kings and queens of England have kept swans for almost 1,000 years. Over 800 years ago they were made "royal" birds with legal protection.

Since swans were valuable, people wanted to show whom they belonged to. They cut identification patterns into their bills with a sharp knife. This is called swan upping. It probably doesn't hurt them. Any swan that didn't have a mark on its bill was claimed by the king or queen of the time. The ceremony of swan upping still takes place every year on the Thames River in England.

# Partners for Life

Opposite page:
*When they are about two years old, male and female mute swans mate and begin to form strong partnerships.*

Male swans are called cobs. Females are called pens. Cobs and pens take their time to decide on a mate; but when they do pair up, it is for life. Since most swans live 10 to 20 years, this is a long-term partnership. Swan pairs are not just loyal to each other for the breeding season when they bring up young. They stay with each other all year and even migrate together.

Mute swans start practicing their mating behaviors when they are young. They practice even before they have replaced all their gray feathers with the white grown-up feathers. Young swans greet each other by turning their heads from side to side. When they are about two years old, males and females start to form very close relationships. About a year later a couple will mate for real, build a nest, and then raise baby swans, which are called cygnets. Young male and female tundra swans wait even longer before having a family. They may be five or six years old before having their first babies.

## Showing Off

Starting a family is a major task for a pair of swans. Making sure the eggs hatch safely and that the baby swans grow big and strong is a lot of work. The mom does more than the dad, but both do their part. So before they mate, the two partners display to each other to show that they are serious about the whole thing.

The trumpeter swans' display is the most impressive. The two birds face each other and stretch up their necks. They then half open their wings and shake them vigorously. At the same time, they bend their necks and call loudly. At first, each swan calls separately, but after a few seconds both call together. Finally, they stretch their necks straight out in front.

Practice displays may start well before the swans are adults. Once fully grown, swans pair up properly, though they may be "engaged" for a year before they mate. During mating the male's sperm (sex cells) passes into the female's body and fertilizes (fuses with) her eggs. She lays the fertilized eggs shortly after.

*Opposite page: A male trumpeter swan shakes his wings in a spectacular display in Yellowstone National Park.*

# Building a Home

Opposite page: *Mute swans build a big mound for their nest from bits of water plants. They then line it with feathers and down.*

Laying eggs can be a troublesome business. For a start, eggs are easily broken and need to be given as much protection as possible. Like other birds, swans build a nest to protect them; but unlike most other birds' nests, those of swans can be huge. They have to be, since they are built next to lakes or rivers. If a sudden rainstorm raised water levels, the eggs could be washed away. So swans nest on mounds of plant material raised high above the water.

Male trumpeter swans gather marsh plants like sedges and bulrushes and bring them to the female, who puts them on the nest mound. It takes the couple about two weeks of hard labor to complete the nest. The finished nest may be 12 feet (4 meters) across and 18 inches (0.5 meters) high. The swans may use the same site for several years. Sometimes swans may build their nests close together in colonies. Coscoroba swans' nests may be just out of pecking distance of each other.

# Eggs

In April or May, when the weather is getting warmer and food is easier to find, the mother-to-be lays her eggs. The number of eggs varies according to the type of swan. Mute swans lay between five and eight eggs. They are rounded at both ends and colored pale green. Inside each egg is a tiny embryo, or developing chick. It will only grow big and strong enough to hatch if it is kept warm.

Like most birds, the mother swan sits on the eggs to warm them. This is called incubation. The eggs have to be strong, or they would crack under her weight. The mother regularly turns the eggs so the warmth of her body is evenly spread through each one. With all this fidgeting the eggs get scratched and stained with brown and yellow lines and blotches.

Each developing chick grows an egg tooth. It is not really a tooth but a little hook on its beak. After about 40 days the chick uses this tooth to smash its way out of the egg—and into the outside world.

Opposite page:
*A mother mute swan sits on her clutch of eggs to keep them warm. The eggs vary in color from pale gray to pale blue.*

# Chicks

Opposite page:
*When they hatch, baby swans look like ducklings. They have short necks and are covered in brown or gray down.*

Newly hatched swan chicks are tiny balls of fluff—not white like mom and dad, but soft gray. The little chicks, called cygnets, don't have real feathers but fluffy down. Swans' down is so warm it is highly prized for filling quilts. A cygnet's soft down feathers keep it snug but aren't strong enough for flight.

For the first 10 days of their lives baby mute swans often ride on their mother's back. They can swim, and they also have a strong urge to climb. If mom lifts her foot, the cygnets climb onto it and jump up on her back. Sometimes dad gives a piggyback instead.

Cygnets are not too good at feeding themselves. So their parents collect bits of plant material and drop them close by. The parents also paddle their feet back and forth in the water to stir up food for their infants.

# Growing Up

The cygnets grow quickly, but they are not strong enough to fly until they are between four and five months old. Young swans have gray feathers, so it is always possible to tell them from the grownups. Even after they are old enough to fly, they still show a blotchy gray color. Tundra swan families tend to stick together for a long time.

When the swans are ready to fly south in the fall, they make signals to all the family members so everyone knows it's time to get ready. There may be up to five youngsters in every family, though usually there are fewer. The swans bob their heads up and down to each other, bending and stretching their necks and calling loudly. Mom and dad stick with the young swans when they fly south, then watch out for them through the winter. Parent swans make their young fend for themselves when they are about one year old.

# Words to Know

**Aquatic**  Describing animals or plants that live in water.

**Clutch**  A batch of eggs laid at the same time by one mother.

**Cob**  Male swan.

**Courtship**  The way male and female swans and other animals attract each other before mating.

**Cygnet**  Young swan.

**Fertilization**  The joining of a sperm (male sex cell) and egg (female sex cell) to make a single cell that will grow into a unique individual.

**Invertebrate**  Animal without a backbone.

**Mate**  To produce young.

**Molt**  When a bird sheds its old feathers so new ones can grow in their place.

**Pen**  Female swan.

**Plumage**  A bird's feathers.

**Preening**  When a bird cleans its feathers with its beak and oils them to keep them in good condition.

**Prey**  The animals that another animal eats.

**Species**  A particular type of animal.

**Webbed**  Describing the skin between a swan's toes, used to push against the water to help the bird move.

# INDEX

**Cover Photo:** Bruce Coleman: Mr P. Clement.

**Photo Credits:** Ardea: John Cancalosi 45, Hans D. Dossenbach 42, Stefan Meyers 33, B. "Moose" Peterson 8; Bruce Coleman: John Cancalosi 4, Allan G. Potts 20/21; NHPA: Joe Blossom 37, Hellio & Van Ingen 25, Andy Rouse 15, Eric Soder 30, R. Sorensen & J. Olsen 22; Oxford Scientific Films: David Cayless 7, Mark Hamblin 29, Roland Mayr 41, Stan Osolinski 12, 38, Chris Perrins 34, Konrad Wothe 11; Still Pictures: Roland Seitre 16, 26.